BEGINNER'S ORIGAMI

All of the works of art reproduced in this book are from the collections of The Metropolitan Museum of Art.

First published in 2003 by The Metropolitan Museum of Art, New York, and Viking, a division of Penguin Putnam
Books for Young Readers, 345 Hudson Street, New York, New York 10014, U.S.A., and Penguin Books Canada, Ltd., 10 Alcorn Avenue,
Toronto, Ontario, Canada, M4V 3B2

First Edition
Printed in Hong Kong
12 11 10 09 08 07 06 05 04 03   5 4 3 2

Produced by the Department of Special Publications, The Metropolitan Museum of Art:
Robie Rogge, Publishing Manager; Judith Cressy, Project Editor; Victoria Gallina, Production Associate.

Photography by The Metropolitan Museum of Art Photograph Studio unless otherwise noted.
Photography of the origami models by Nancy Lund.

Designed by Miriam Berman.

Visit the Museum's Web site: www.metmuseum.org
Visit Viking's Web site: www.penguinputnam.com

ISBN 1-58839-027-6 (MMA)
ISBN 0-670-03648-X (Viking)

BEGINNER'S ORIGAMI

BIRDS, BEASTS, BUGS, & BUTTERFLIES

by Steve and Megumi Biddle

THE METROPOLITAN MUSEUM OF ART

VIKING

Contents

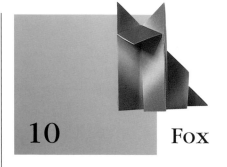
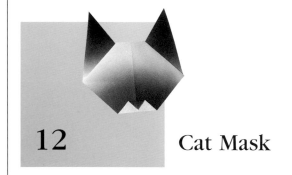
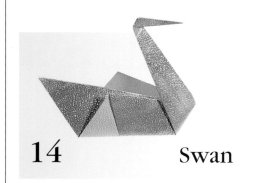

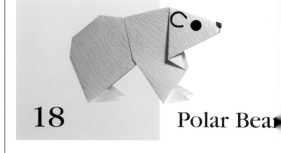
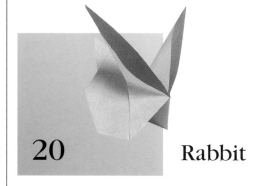
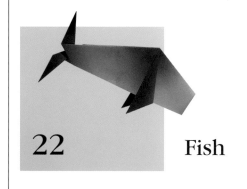
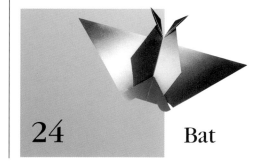

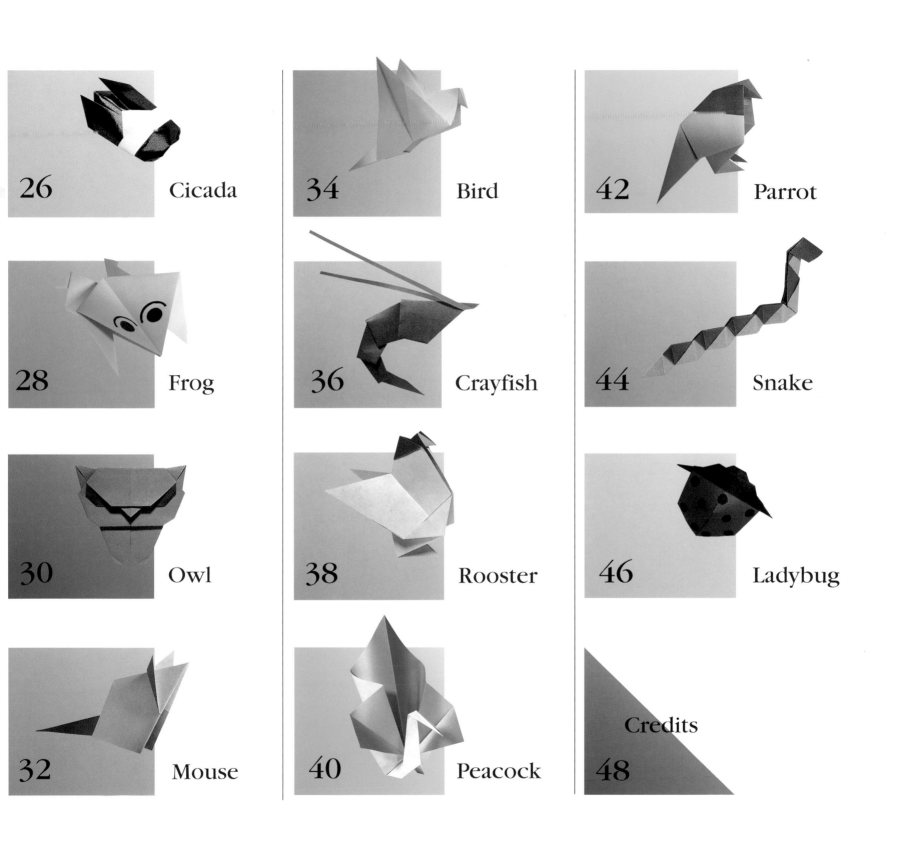

Introduction

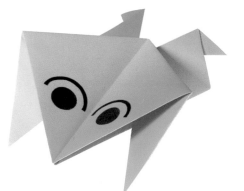

Nature and all of its creatures are traditional themes in origami, but the birds, beasts, bugs, and butterflies in this book were inspired not by nature itself but by animals that creep, crawl, swim, and fly in works of art in the collections of The Metropolitan Museum of Art. The images were drawn from both Asian and Western sources, reflecting origami's adaptability and widespread appeal.

People have been folding paper ever since it was invented in China in A.D. 105. But it was in Japan, during the Edo period (1615–1868), when paper finally became inexpensive enough for everyone to use, that origami became a form of entertainment. The various ways of folding paper to make animals, flowers, and other things, both simple and complex, were passed down by parents to their children for generations until modern times. Beginning in the 1890s, the Japanese government established a widespread system of preschool education, and origami was introduced as a tool for coordinating young minds and hands. Since the 1950s, interest in origami has grown in the United States, Great Britain, and Europe, as well as in Japan. Origami is as intriguing to adults as it is to children, and there are challenges to be had at all levels of expertise. This book has been created especially for beginners. Each of the twenty origami models on these pages can be made in ten steps or fewer, and they are arranged in order of difficulty. If you have never done origami before, start with the simple butterfly on page 8, then gradually work your way through to the end of the book, finishing with the ladybug on page 46. You will no longer be a beginner when you have completed all the models.

The pocket on the front of this book contains traditional origami paper, colored on one side and white on the other. You can purchase additional packets of paper at stationery stores, Asian gift shops, toy stores, and arts and crafts supply stores. Part of the fun of origami is choosing what type of paper to fold. For paper with texture or a decorative surface, cut your own squares from specialty paper found at art supply shops. For beautifully patterned paper, do the same with gift wrap from stationery stores. You can use writing paper, computer paper, even pages cut from a magazine. In fact, all kinds of paper can be used for origami.

Most of the models in this book start out with a single square of paper. For some of the projects you will also need a tube of glue, a felt-tip pen, or a pair of scissors. The instructions that introduce each project indicate what materials are required.

To learn more about origami, you can contact the following organizations: O.U.S.A. Center of America, 15 West 77th Street, New York, New York 10024-5192
Web site: www.origami-usa.org

The Membership Secretary, British Origami Society, 2a The Chestnuts, Countesthorpe, Leicestershire LE8 5TL, England
Web site: www.britishorigami.org.uk

The Nippon Origami Association, 2-064 Domir Gobancho, 12 Gobancho Chiyoda-ku, Tokyo, 102-0076, Japan
Web site: www.origami-noa.com

We would like to thank John Cunliffe, Kunihiko Kasahara, Mitsuo Okuda, Takenao Handa, and our friends in the Nippon Origami Association for their help and support with *Beginner's Origami: Birds, Beasts, Bugs, & Butterflies.*

—Steve and Megumi Biddle

Helpful Hints

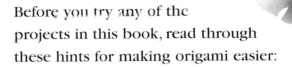

Before you try any of the projects in this book, read through these hints for making origami easier:

■   Use a piece of paper with a color or pattern that will be ideal for the model you are going to make.

■   If you are using your own paper rather than that supplied with this book, make sure it is cut absolutely square. There is nothing more frustrating than trying to fold a nearly square square!

■   Fold on a smooth, flat surface such as a table or a book. Make neat, accurate folds.

■   Press each fold into place by smoothing it with your thumbnail. Do not panic if your first few attempts at folding are not very successful. With practice you will understand the various ways a piece of paper behaves when it is folded.

■   Look at each diagram carefully, read the instructions, then look ahead to the next diagram to see what shape will be created when you have completed the step you are working on. Note that in the diagrams, the shading represents the colored side of the paper.

■   Above all, if you are finding a particular fold tricky, do not give up! Just put the model aside and come back to it another day with a fresh mind.

PAPILIO ERITHONIUS.

Collectors' card from the series
Butterflies and Moths of America
L. Prang and Co., lithographers, American, ca. 1864

For the **butterfly,**
use one square of paper,
white side up.

Butterfly

The beautifully colored
and patterned wings of butterflies have fascinated artists all
over the world. Most often
butterflies are depicted with
flowers, where they alight to
feed on nectar. Butterflies are
among the delights of the
summer garden.

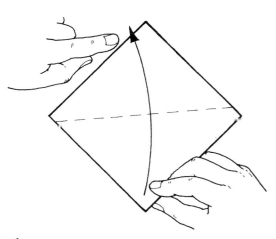

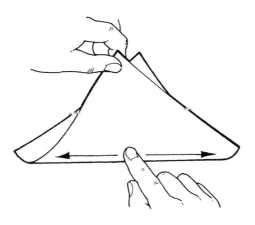

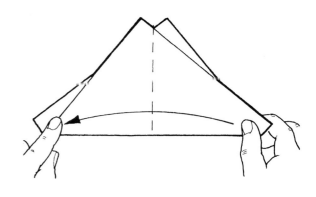

1 Turn the square around to look like a diamond. Fold the bottom corner up . . .

2 on a slant. Press firmly along the bottom edge.

3 Fold in half from right to left.

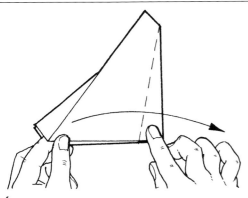

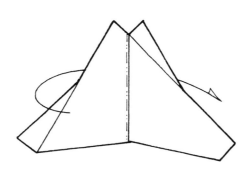

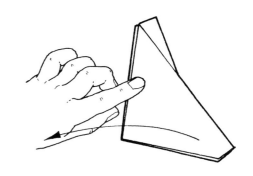

4 Fold one flap of paper over to the right, as shown. Do the same . . .

5 with the flap behind.

6 Press firmly; then pull the flaps apart . . .

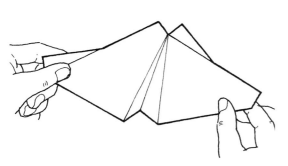

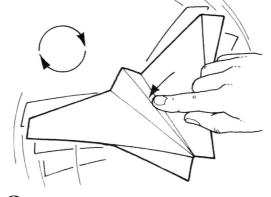

7 to make the wings.

8 To complete the butterfly, turn the paper around. Lightly tap the butterfly's body to make its wings flutter.

Choose brightly colored paper to make a vivid butterfly.

9

*F*or the **fox,**
*use one square of paper,
white side up.*

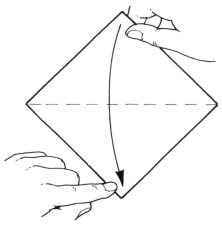

1 Turn the square around to look like a diamond. Fold in half from top to bottom.

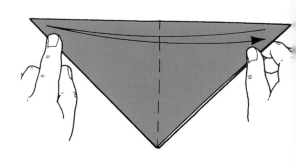

2 Fold and unfold in half from side to side.

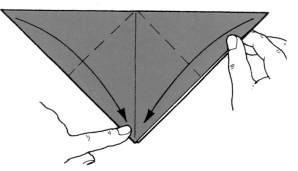

3 Fold the top points down to the bottom point.

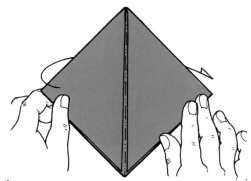

4 Fold in half behind, from side to side.

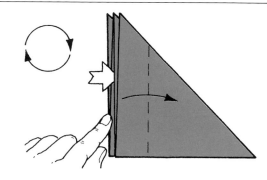

5 Turn the paper around. Pull the layers apart at the side, as shown, and . . .

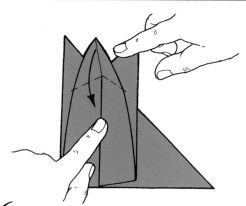

6 flatten the middle point down to make the head.

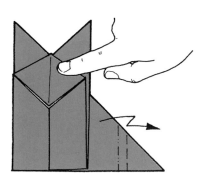

7 Fold the right point backward and forward to make the tail.

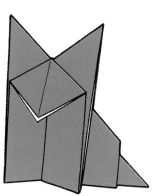

8 Here is the completed fox.

Fox

Fox Jumping *(detail)*
Kyōsai (Kawanabe Shūsaburo), Japanese, 1831–1889

In this animated painting, the fox looks ready to leap, his paws poised for pouncing on his dinner, a smaller animal perhaps. When seated, as in our origami model, a fox looks as docile as a pet dog.

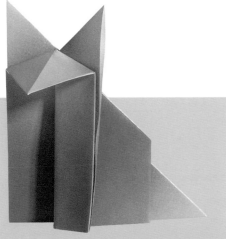

Foxes range in color from white to red to brown to silvery gray. Give some thought to the color of paper you choose for your fox.

11

*For the **cat**, use one square of paper, white side up.*

You will also need some glue.

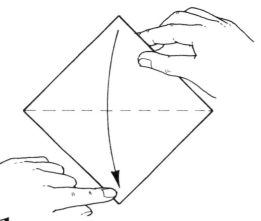

1 Turn the square around to look like a diamond. Fold in half from top to bottom.

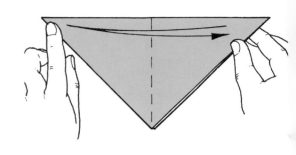

2 Fold and unfold in half from side to side.

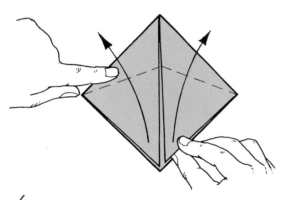

4 Fold the points up to either side of the top point.

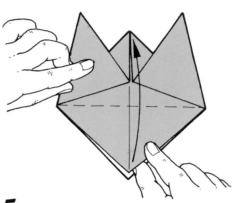

5 Fold one bottom point up as far as possible.

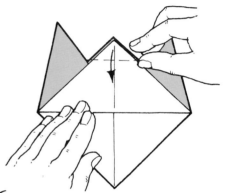

6 Fold the middle points down, as shown.

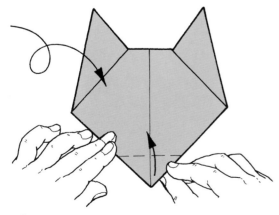

8 Turn the paper over. Fold the bottom point up.

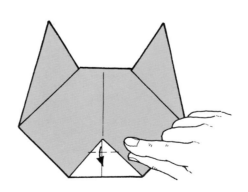

9 Fold the tip of the point down to make the nose.

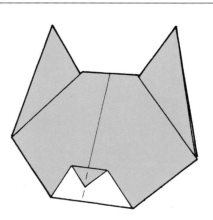

10 Here is the completed cat mask.

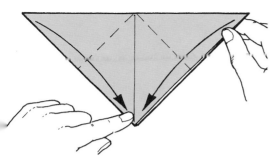

3 Fold the top points down to the bottom point.

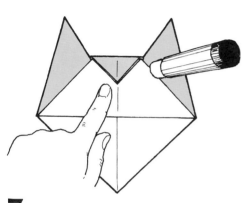

7 Glue the middle points down.

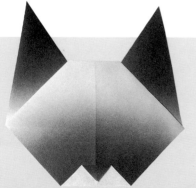

To make a mask to wear, use a 22-inch square of paper. When completed, open out the mask from behind and place it on your head.

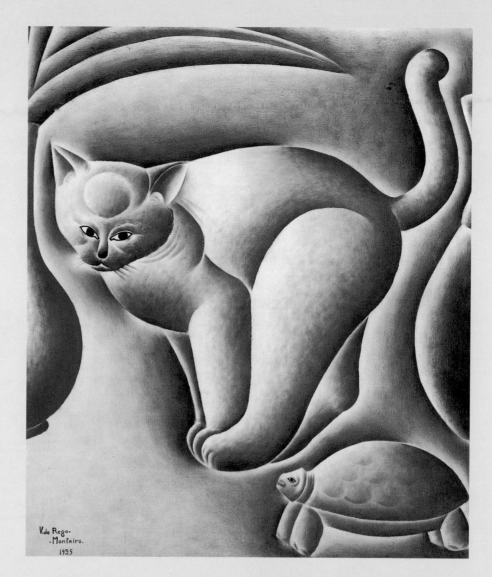

Cat Mask

A pretty face is only one of the reasons that cats have been a popular subject for artists of every era and in all parts of the world. In this painting by a Brazilian artist, the cat has a wary look, as if not sure what to make of the slow-moving turtle.

Cat and Turtle
Vicente de Rego Monteiro, Brazilian, 1899–1970

*For the **swan**, use one square of white paper.*

Swan

Artists often depict swans swimming in pairs, and the Tiffany studio artists who created this mosaic were no exception. In fact, swans are often seen swimming in pairs in the wild, because they mate for life.

Garden Landscape and Fountain *(detail)*
Tiffany Studios, New York City, ca. 1915

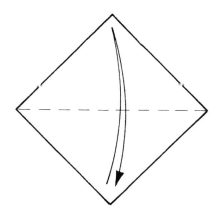

1 Turn the square around to look like a diamond. Fold and unfold in half from bottom to top.

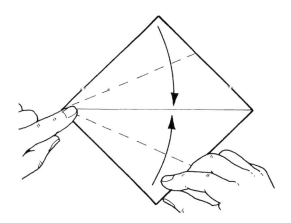

2 From the left point, fold the sloping sides in to meet the middle fold line.

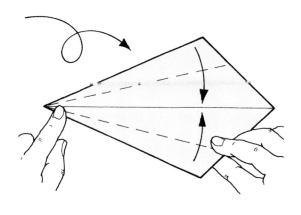

3 Turn the paper over. Again, from the left point, fold the sloping sides in to meet the middle fold line.

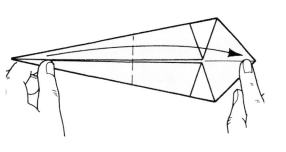

4 Fold the left point over to the right point to make the neck.

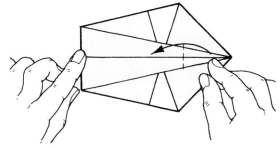

5 Fold the point back over a little to make the head.

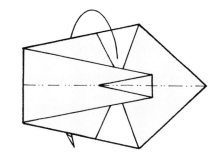

6 Fold the top behind to the bottom.

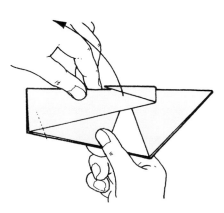

7 Pull the neck up into the position shown in step 8. Press firmly.

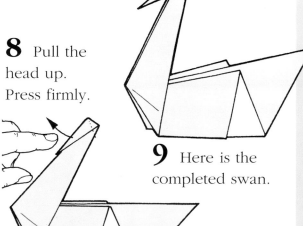

8 Pull the head up. Press firmly.

9 Here is the completed swan.

This graceful swan looks like it is gliding on water.

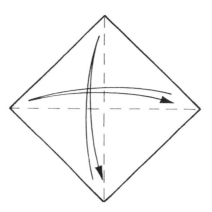

1 Turn the square around to look like a diamond. Fold and unfold the opposite corners together.

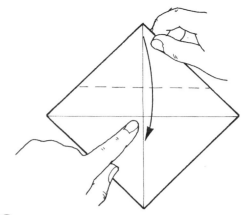

2 Fold the top corner down beyond the middle.

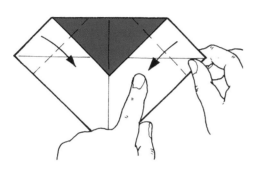

3 Fold the top sloping edges over . . .

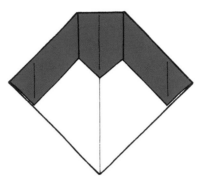

4 as shown. Press firmly.

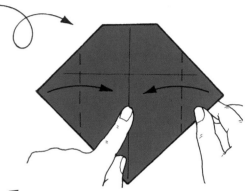

5 Turn the paper over. Fold the side points over toward the middle fold line.

6 Fold the side points out on a slant . . .

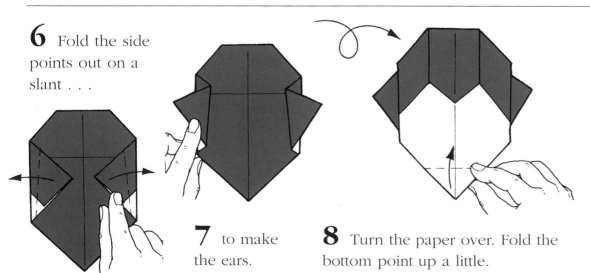

7 to make the ears.

8 Turn the paper over. Fold the bottom point up a little.

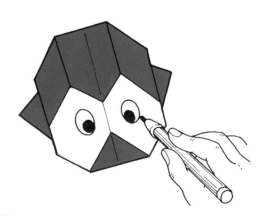

9 To complete the monkey mask, draw eyes with a felt-tip pen.

Three Monkeys *(detail)*
Mori Sosen, Japanese, 1747–1821

Monkey Mask

Many monkeys live in close social groups, adults and children together. The three Japanese monkeys in this painting seem to be cuddling up for a nap. The artist has made their faces wonderfully expressive.

*M*ake several monkey masks and draw different types of eyes on them to give them different expressions.

Polar Bear

This elegant little sculpture presents a very sleek and stylized polar bear, yet still manages to capture the essence of the animal. Polar bears are perfectly adapted to their frozen habitat, with large bodies for warmth, and short legs and big feet for steadiness on icy terrain.

Polar Bear
François Pompon, French, 1855–1933

*F*or *the* **polar bear,** *use two squares of white paper, both the same size.*

You will also need some glue and a felt-tip pen.

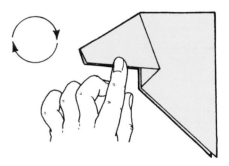

4 To complete, turn the paper around.

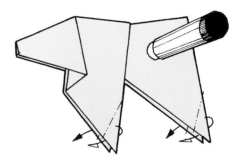

8 a sloping angle. Glue the two sections together. Fold the bottom points, as shown, to make the paws.

1 To make the head and front legs, turn one square around to look like a diamond. Fold in half from bottom to top.

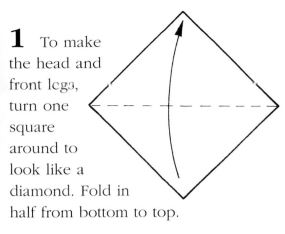

2 Fold the top points down a little. Fold in half from right to left.

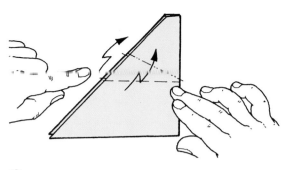

3 Fold the paper on either side, as shown, to make the head.

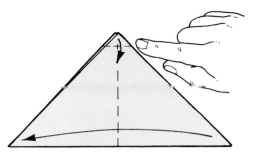

5 To make the back legs, turn the remaining square around to look like a diamond. Fold in half from bottom to top.

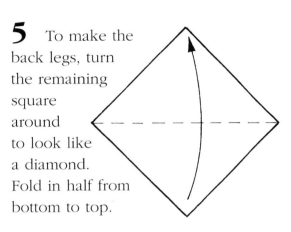

6 Fold in half from right to left.

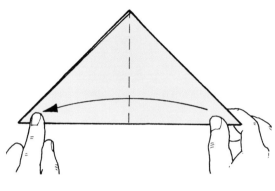

7 To assemble the bear, turn the back legs around. Tuck them into the front legs at . . .

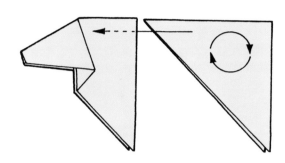

9 Push the top right point down inside the model.

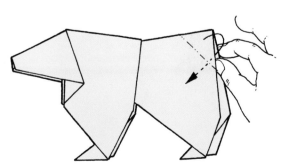

10 To complete the polar bear, draw eyes, nose, and ears with the felt-tip pen.

Make different species of bears by using different shades of paper.

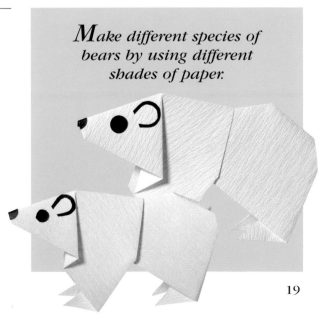

19

Rabbit

Rabbits, like the three in this painting, look so calm when they are busy eating. But their long ears are always alert. With the slightest sound or disturbance, rabbits are off with a bound, fleet runners.

Three Rabbits *(detail)*
Chinese, Qing dynasty (1644–1911)

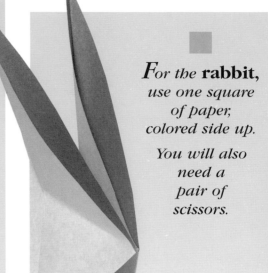

*F*or the **rabbit**, *use one square of paper, colored side up.*

You will also need a pair of scissors.

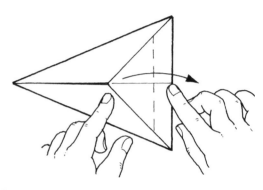

4 back out a little to make the tail.

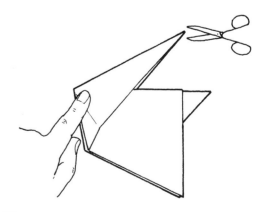

8 From the point's tip, cut along the fold line to make the ears.

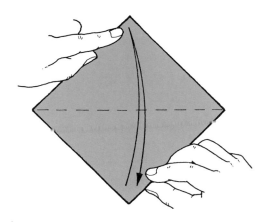

1 Turn the square around to look like a diamond. Fold and unfold in half from bottom to top.

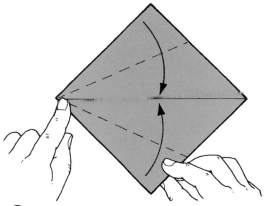

2 From the left point, fold the sloping sides in to meet the middle fold line.

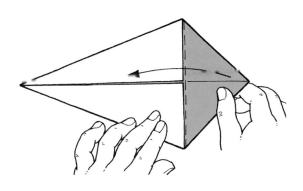

3 Fold the right point over toward the left and . . .

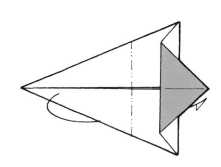

5 Fold in half behind, from side to side.

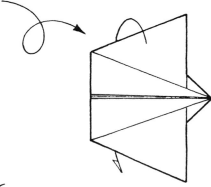

6 Turn the paper over. Fold the top behind to the bottom.

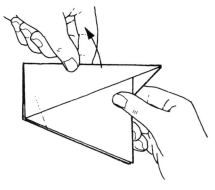

7 Pull the point up into the position shown in step 8. Press firmly.

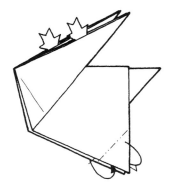

9 Open the ears slightly. Fold the right bottom points up inside the model.

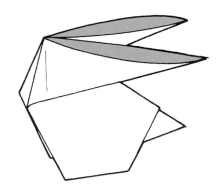

10 Here is the completed rabbit.

By making slight variations in the folds and cuts, you can create a rabbit with small or large ears.

21

*F*or the **fish,** *use one square of paper, white side up.*

You will also need a pair of scissors.

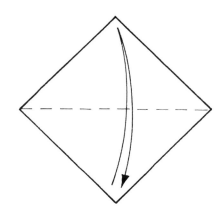

1 Turn the square around to look like a diamond. Fold and unfold in half from bottom to top.

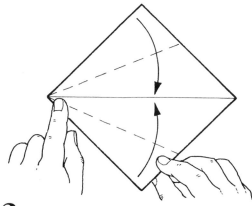

2 From the left point, fold the sloping sides in to meet the middle fold line.

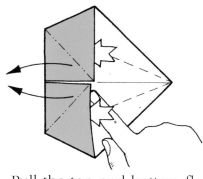

4 Pull the top and bottom flaps of paper over to the left, making their sloping sides come to meet on the middle fold line.

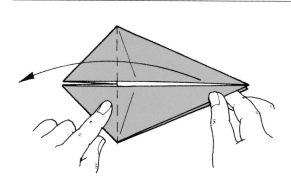

5 Fold one right point over to the left.

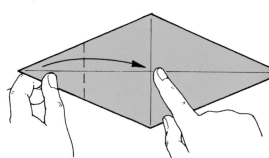

6 Fold the left point in to the midc

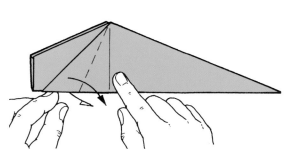

8 Fold the front flap over, as shown, to make a fin. Repeat behind.

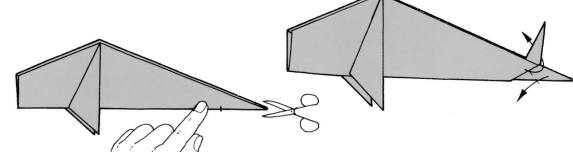

9 From the right point's tip, cut along the fold line a little to make the tail fins.

10 To complete the fish, fold one tail fin up and the other down.

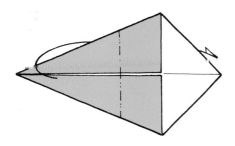

3 Fold in half behind, from side to side.

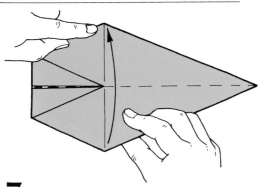

7 Fold the bottom up to the top.

Origami models are most effective when they are displayed together. Why not try making a school of fish?

Fish

The artist Hiroshige made the contrast between two different types of fish very clear in this woodblock print. Fish come in all colors and sizes whether they live in fresh or salt water. Both flounders and rockfish live in the ocean.

Flounder and Rockfish with Cherry Blossoms
Ando Hiroshige, Japanese, 1797–1858

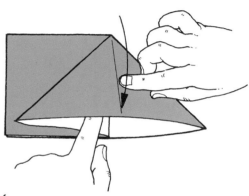

4 and with your free hand, press
it down neatly into a triangle.

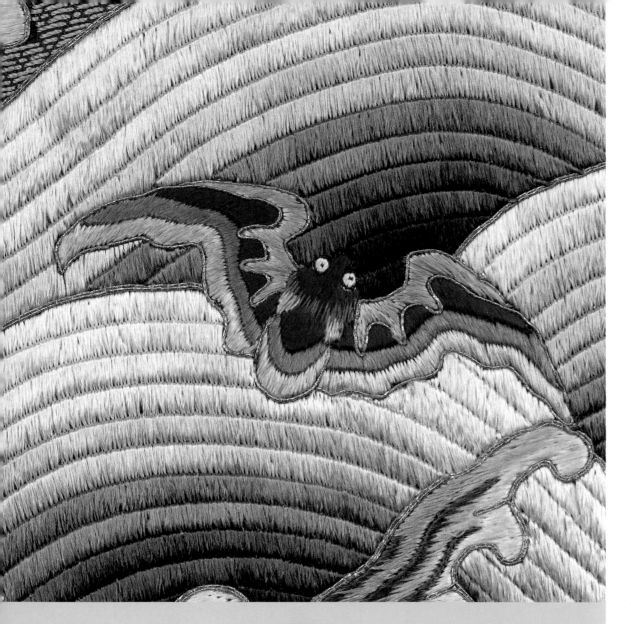

Bat

Bats do not have a very positive reputation in the West,
but in China, they symbolize happiness. That is because the
word for bat sounds like the word for happiness in Chinese.

Detail of an emperor's twelve-symbol robe
Chinese, 18th century

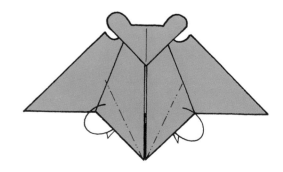

8 the head. Fold the bottom
points in half behind to make the feet

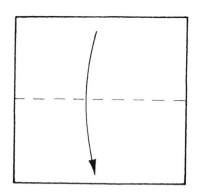

1 Fold the square in half from top to bottom.

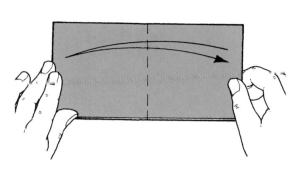

2 Fold and unfold in half from side to side.

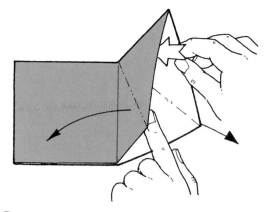

3 Lift one half up along the middle fold line. Start to open out the paper . . .

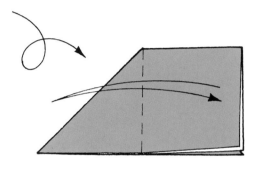

5 Turn the paper over. Repeat steps 2 through 4.

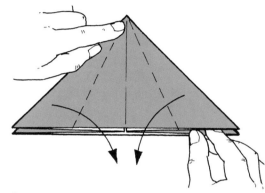

6 From the top point, fold the topmost sloping sides over to meet the middle fold line.

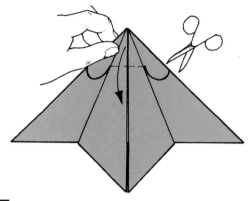

7 Carefully cut two rounded ear shapes as shown. Fold the top point down to make . . .

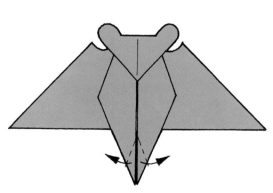

9 Fold the tips of the feet out to either side.

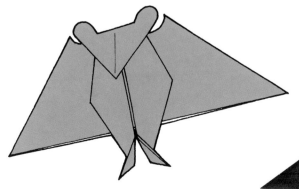

10 Here is the completed bat.

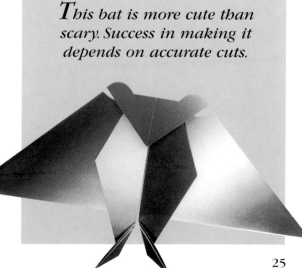

This bat is more cute than scary. Success in making it depends on accurate cuts.

25

For the **cicada,** *use one square of paper, white side up.*

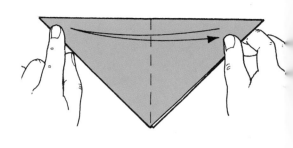

1 Turn the square around to look like a diamond. Fold in half from top to bottom.

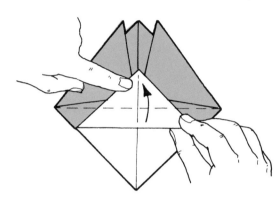

2 Fold and unfold in half from side to side.

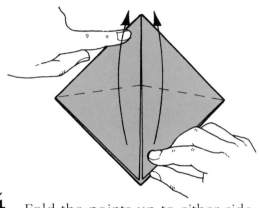

4 Fold the points up to either side of the top point.

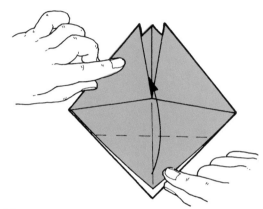

5 Fold one bottom point up beyond the middle to make a triangle.

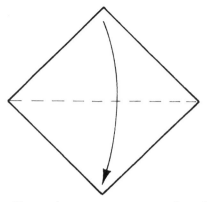

6 Fold the triangle's bottom edge up, as shown.

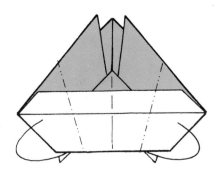

8 Fold the side points behind so that they overlap slightly.

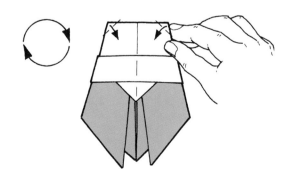

9 Turn the paper around. Fold the top points over a little to make the eyes.

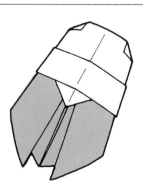

10 Here is the completed cicada.

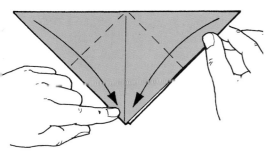

3 Fold the top points down to the bottom point.

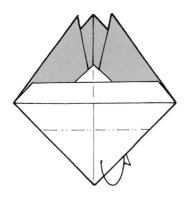

7 Fold the remaining bottom point behind.

The cicada is an insect that makes a shrill singing noise.

Cicada

This woodblock print by the Japanese artist Utamaro shows a cicada alighting on a squash in the height of the summer growing season. Cicadas are a familiar insect in many areas during the summer months, recognizable by their stout bodies, blunt heads, and large, transparent wings.

Grasshopper and Cicada *(detail)*
Kitagawa Utamaro, Japanese, 1754–1806

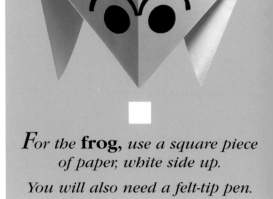

*F*or the **frog,** use a square piece of paper, white side up.

You will also need a felt-tip pen.

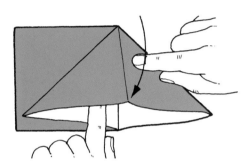

4   and with your free hand press it down neatly into a triangle.

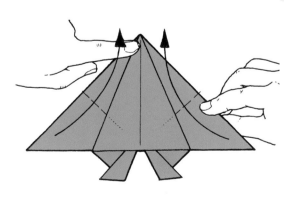

8   Fold the bottom points up to . . .

Frog

The Chinese artist who made this painting caught a frog at one of its most characteristic moments. Flying insects are among the things that frogs like to eat, and this frog has got his eye on one.

Frog on a Lotus Leaf
Xiang Shengmou, Chinese, 1597–1658

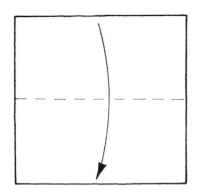

1 Fold the square in half from top to bottom.

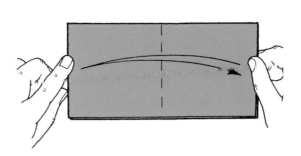

2 Fold and unfold in half from side to side.

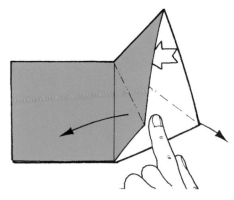

3 Lift one half up along the middle fold line. Start to open out the paper . . .

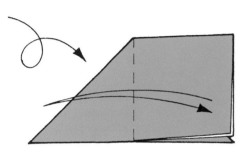

5 Turn the paper over. Repeat steps 2 through 4.

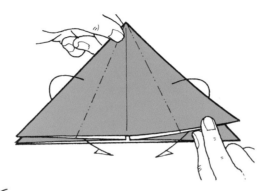

6 From the top point, fold the topmost sloping sides behind to meet the middle fold line.

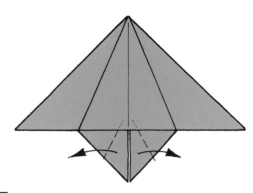

7 Fold the bottom points out to either side.

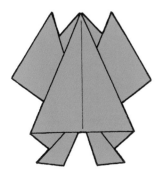

9 either side of the top point.

10 Turn the paper over. To complete the frog, draw eyes with the felt-tip pen.

The frog will have a realistic look if you make it with green paper.

29

For the **owl**, *use one square of paper, white side up.*

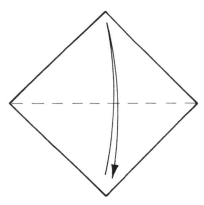

1 Turn the square around to look like a diamond. Fold and unfold in half from bottom to top.

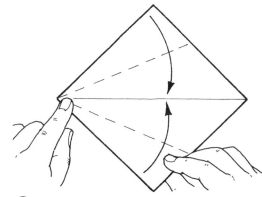

2 From the left point, fold the sloping sides in to meet the middle fold line.

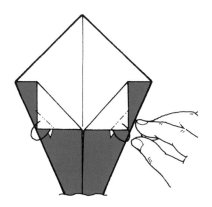

4 Fold the tips of the eyes behind.

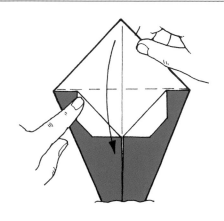

5 Fold the top point down over the eyes.

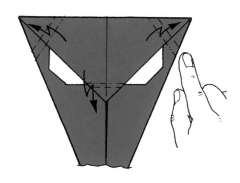

6 Fold the top and middle points backward and forward, as shown.

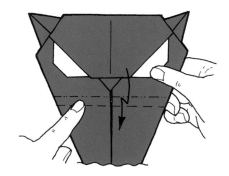

8 Fold the paper backward and forward, as shown.

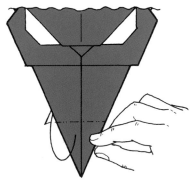

9 Fold the bottom point behind.

10 To complete the owl, fold the side points behind and the bottom points forward.

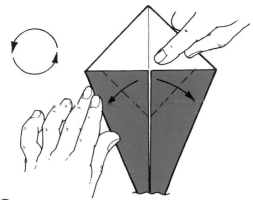

3 Turn the paper around. Fold the two middle points out to either side to make the eyes.

7 Fold the top edge behind.

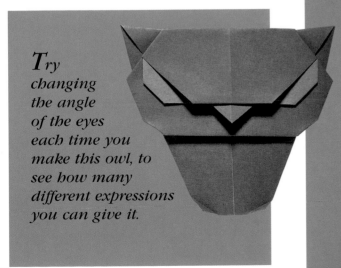

Try changing the angle of the eyes each time you make this owl, to see how many different expressions you can give it.

Owl

As the artist who made this golden owl must have been aware, an owl's eyes are among its most amazing characteristics. Owls are birds of prey, and their large eyes allow them to function successfully at night when they do their hunting.

Finial
Colombian, Sinu, 5th to 10th century

Mouse

Three little mice are doing their best to destroy a folding fan on this Japanese lacquer box. Much to people's chagrin, mice excel at making a meal out of household goods. Their keen eyesight, minute size, and clever paws give them expertise at getting into small places, and their sharp teeth are especially designed for gnawing.

Detail of a writing box
Ogawa Haritsu, Japanese, 1663–1747

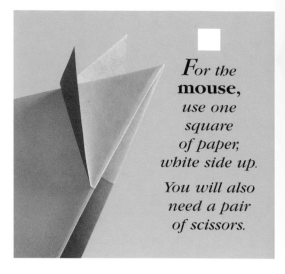

*F*or the **mouse,** *use one square of paper, white side up.*

You will also need a pair of scissors.

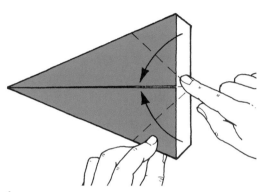

4 Fold each half of the right side in to meet the middle line.

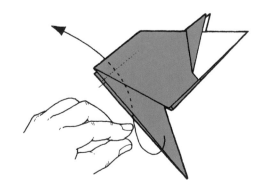

8 back out, as shown, to make the tail.

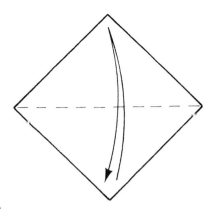

1 Turn the square around to look like a diamond. Fold and unfold in half from bottom to top.

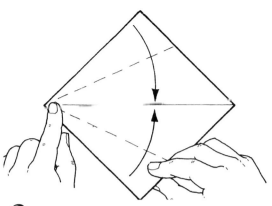

2 From the left point, fold the sloping sides in to meet the middle fold line.

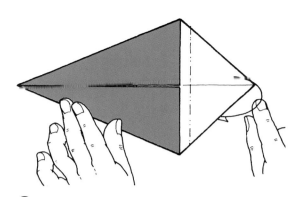

3 Fold the right point behind, as shown.

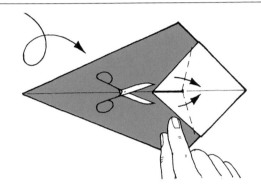

5 Turn the paper over. Cut along the fold line, as shown, to make the ears. Fold the ears over.

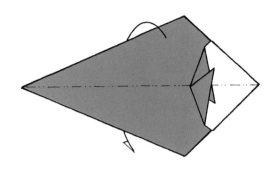

6 Fold the top behind to the bottom.

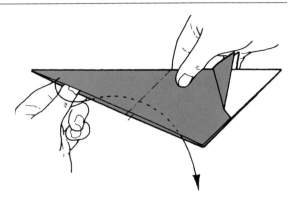

7 Push the left point down inside the model and . . .

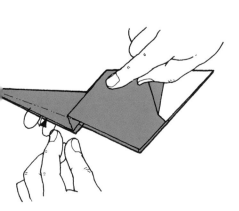

9 Fold the tail's sloping sides up inside the model.

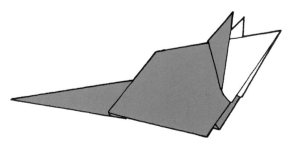

10 Here is the completed mouse.

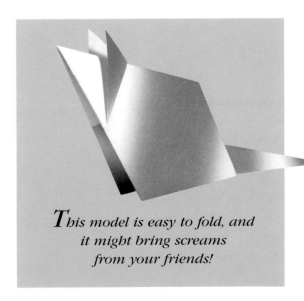

This model is easy to fold, and it might bring screams from your friends!

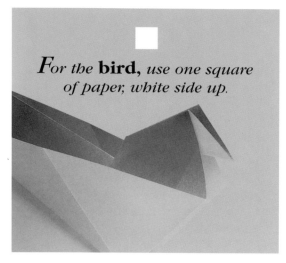

For the **bird**, *use one square of paper, white side up.*

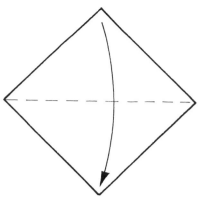

1 Turn the square around to look like a diamond. Fold in half from top to bottom.

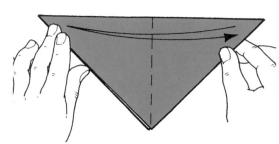

2 Fold and unfold in half from side to side.

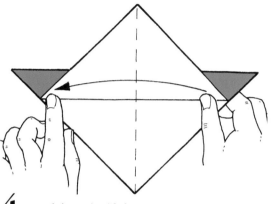

4 Fold in half from right to left.

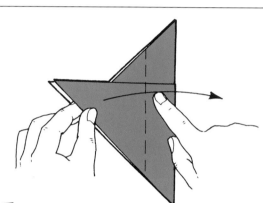

5 Fold one flap of paper over to the right.

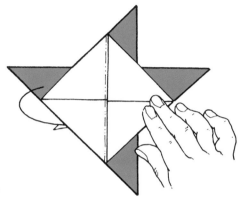

6 Repeat step 5 behind.

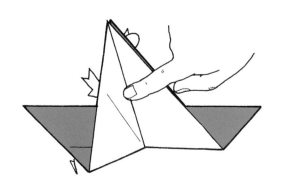

8 as shown, to make a wing. Repeat behind.

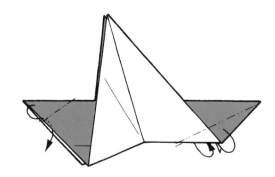

9 Fold the right sloping sides up inside the model to make the tail. Push the left point down inside the model to make the head.

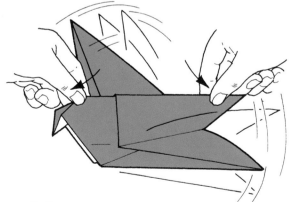

10 Here is the completed bird. Hold the bird's head, pull the tail, and the wings will flap!

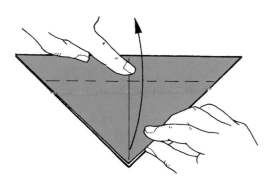

3 Fold one bottom point up beyond the top edge.

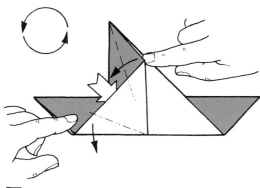

7 Turn the paper around. Open out the left sloping side and pull it downward . . .

This bird's wings flap so well it just might fly away!

Bird

Spring, the time when many blossoms come into bloom, is a busy time for songbirds. First they have to gather materials to build their nests where they lay their eggs. When the eggs are hatched, the adults are even busier, finding food and feeding their young.

Birds and Flowers
Watanabe Seitei, Japanese, 1851–1918

Crayfish
Watanabe Seitei, Japanese, 1851–1918

For the **crayfish,**
*use one square
of paper,
white side up.*
*You will also need a
pair of scissors.*

Crayfish

In looking at the creature in this painting you might think that it is a lobster. And you would be right. Crayfish are small lobsters that live in fresh water, while large lobsters live in the sea. Crayfish can be found in rivers, streams, and swamps, where they are apt to hide behind rocks and logs so that they can surprise their prey.

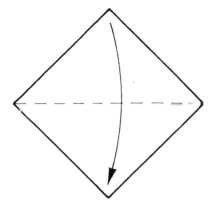

1 Turn the square around to look like a diamond. Fold in half from top to bottom.

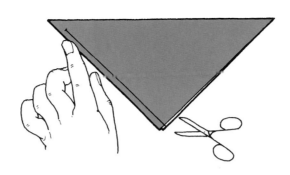

2 Cut along the line, as shown, to make the antennae. Carefully open out the paper from bottom to top.

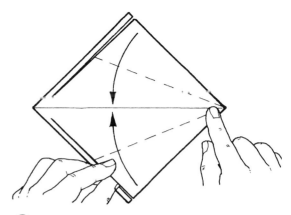

3 From the right point, fold the sloping sides in to meet the middle fold line.

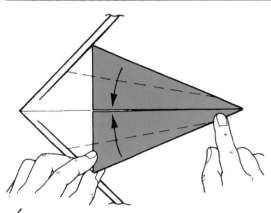

4 Starting short of the right point, fold the sloping sides toward the middle line to make the body.

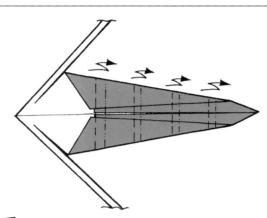

5 Fold the body forward and backward repeatedly, as shown, to make pleats.

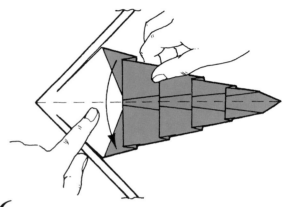

6 Fold in half from top to bottom.

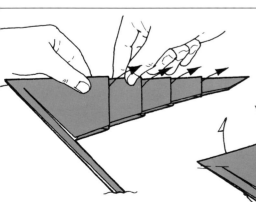

7 Pull the pleats made in step 5 out slightly to curve the body.

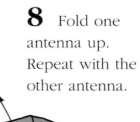

8 Fold one antenna up. Repeat with the other antenna.

9 Here is the completed crayfish.

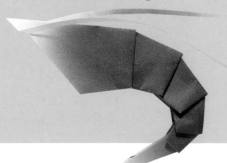

Once you have perfected folding this model, try folding it out of shiny metallic foil, which will help the crayfish hold its shape.

*F*or the **rooster,** use one square of paper, colored side up.

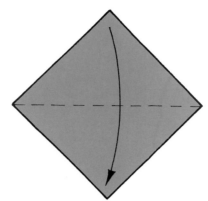

1 Turn the square around to look like a diamond. Fold in half from top to bottom.

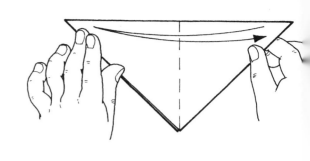

2 Fold and unfold in half from side to side.

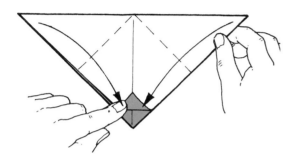

4 Fold the top points down to the bottom point.

5 Fold in half behind, from side to side.

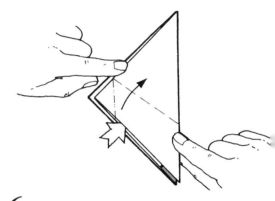

6 Fold the front flap of paper over, as shown . . .

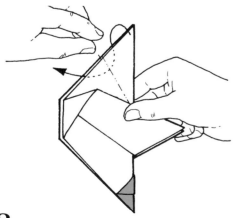

8 Push the top point down inside the model to make the feet.

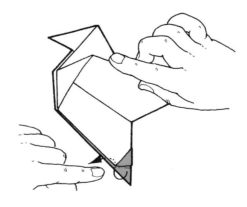

9 Push the bottom point up inside the model to make the beak.

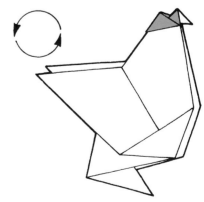

10 To complete the rooster, turn the paper around.

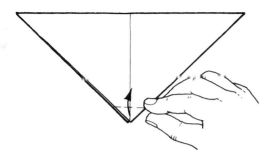

3   Fold one bottom point up a little.

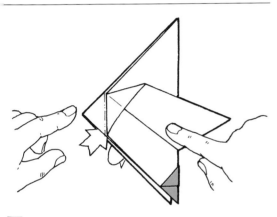

7   flattening down the side point into a triangle. Repeat steps 6 and 7 behind.

Try changing the angle of the head and wings each time you fold this model to see how many different roosters you can make.

Rooster

The American artist Milton Avery was a master at painting abstract scenes that are playful and colorful, and that convey their subject perfectly. He ingeniously used simple forms to create the convincing rooster and hens in this painting.

White Rooster
Milton Avery, American, 1885–1965

Peacock

The glittering, iridescent feathers of the peacock make it one of the wonders of the avian world. Peacocks frequently appear in the colorful garden settings of Indian miniature paintings. In this painting, the Hindu god Krishna is surrounded by peacocks and even wears a peacock skirt.

Krishna Fluting (detail)
Indian, Rajasthan, probably Amber, ca. 1610

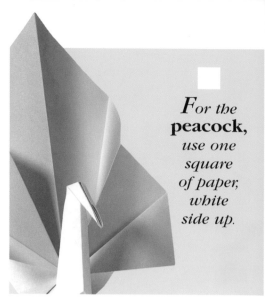

*F*or the **peacock,** use one square of paper, white side up.

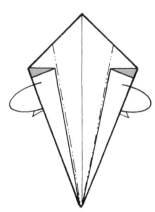

4 From the bottom point, fold the sloping sides behind to meet the middle fold line.

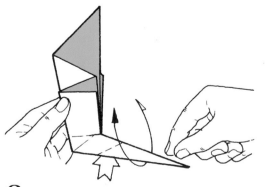

8 as far as possible. Turn the point inside out, as shown, to make the neck.

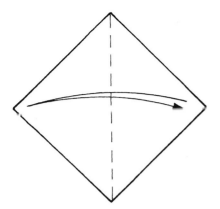

1 Turn the square around to look like a diamond. Fold and unfold in half from side to side.

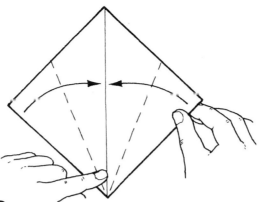

2 From the bottom point, fold the sloping sides in to meet the middle fold line.

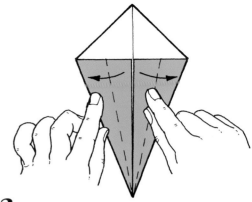

3 Fold the middle edges out as shown.

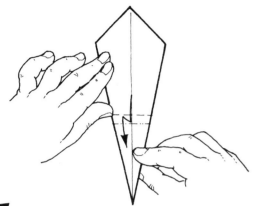

5 Fold the bottom point forward and backward, as shown.

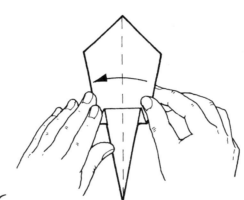

6 Fold the paper in half from right to left.

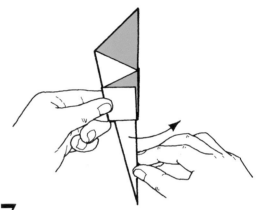

7 Pull the bottom point up . . .

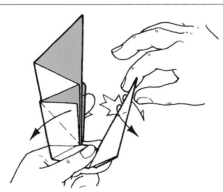

9 Fold the top layer of paper over on a slant, as shown, to make the tail. Repeat behind. Turn the neck's tip inside out to make the head.

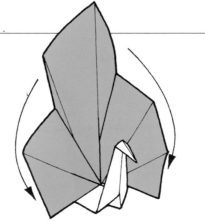

10 To complete the peacock, open out the tail and shape it into place.

The peacock makes a wonderful table decoration when it is folded from a square of colorful gift wrap.

For the **parrot,** *use one square of paper, white side up.*

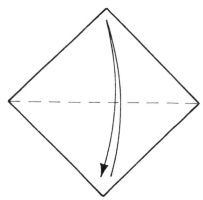

1 Turn the square around to look like a diamond. Fold and unfold in half from bottom to top.

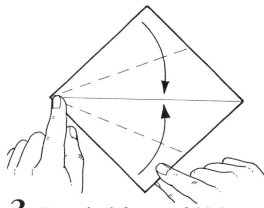

2 From the left point, fold the sloping sides in to meet the middle fold line.

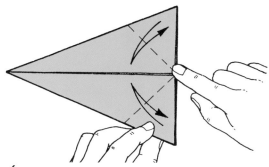

4 Fold each half of the right side in to meet the middle line. Press firmly and open up.

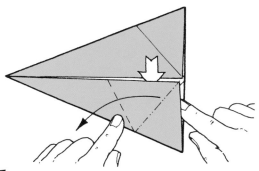

5 Using the fold line made in step 4 as a guide, open out the bottom layer of paper, as shown. Press it down . . .

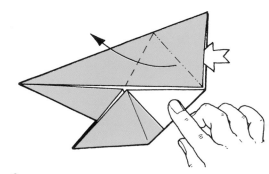

6 into a point. Repeat steps 5 and 6 with the top layer of paper.

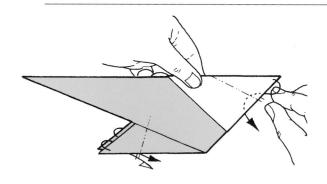

8 Push the right point down inside the model to make the head. Fold the bottom points over toward the right to make the feet.

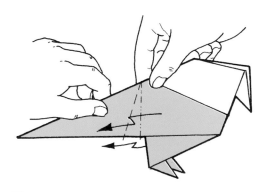

9 Fold the paper on either side, as shown, to make the tail.

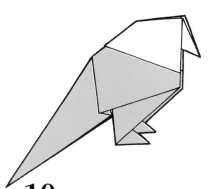

10 Here is the completed parrot.

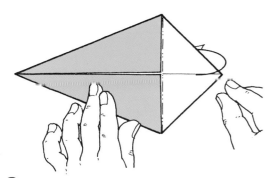

3 Fold the right point behind as shown.

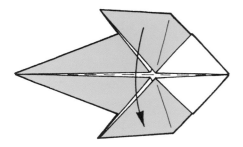

7 Fold in half from top to bottom.

This colorful parrot stands on its own and looks as though it's ready to walk across the table.

Parrot

Parrots are the favorite birds of many people. The way the birds move their heads and walk makes them appear like little people dressed up in exotic costumes. Parrots' colorful plumage gives them great appeal as well, as the stained-glass artist Louis Comfort Tiffany surely would have agreed.

Hibiscus and Parrots (*detail*)
Tiffany Studios, New York City, ca. 1910–20

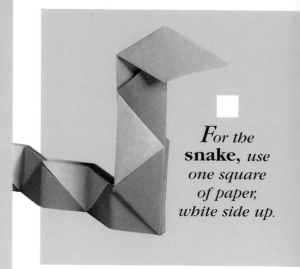

For the **snake,** *use one square of paper, white side up.*

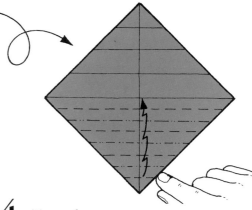

4 Turn the paper over. From the bottom corner, pleat the paper into equal sections, as shown.

Snake

With its tongue darting out and its body arched and curved, this snake looks like it is about to pounce on its prey. Because people tend to be afraid of these reptiles, they usually do not take time to admire the snake's beauty and grace of movement in its natural setting.

Rat Snake with Dayflower Plant *(detail)*
Kitagawa Utamaro, Japanese, 1754–1806

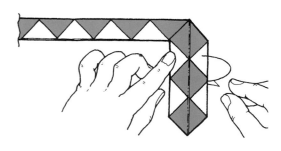

8 into a flap, as shown. Fold the flap in half behind, from side to side.

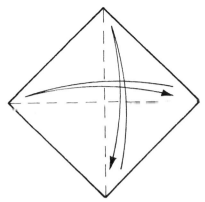

1 Turn the square around to look like a diamond. Fold and unfold the opposite corners together.

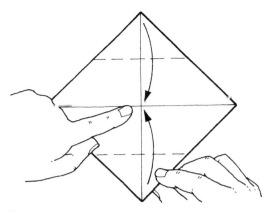

2 Fold the top and bottom corners in to the middle.

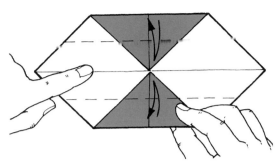

3 Fold the top and bottom edges in to meet the middle fold line. Open up the paper completely.

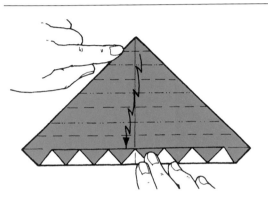

5 From the top corner, pleat the paper into equal sections, as shown. Take care to make the folds neatly.

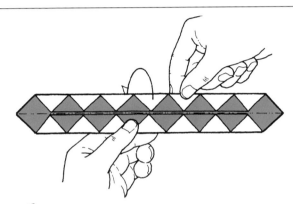

6 Fold the top behind to the bottom to make the body.

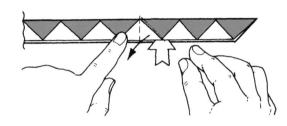

7 Open out the body's right point and press it down neatly . . .

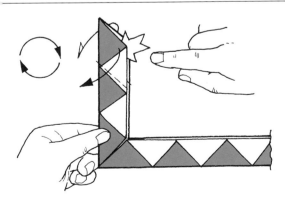

9 Turn the paper around. Turn the flap's tip inside out to make the head.

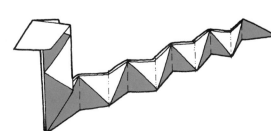

10 To complete the snake, fold the body forward and backward, as shown.

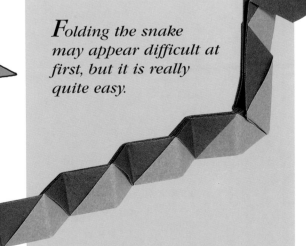

Folding the snake may appear difficult at first, but it is really quite easy.

45

*F*or the **ladybug,** *use one square of paper, white side up.*

You will also need a felt-tip pen.

Ladybug

The ladybug, or ladybird beetle, is one insect that people love to have in their gardens. With their bright red polka-dotted wings, they are pretty little creatures. The ladybug's upper wings meet in a straight line down the center back and act as armor. The Swiss jeweler who made this watch caught the ladybug's style admirably.

Watch
Swiss, mid-19th century

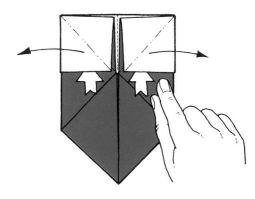

4 Pull the top layers of paper out to either side, pressing them down . . .

8 Fold the middle point's tip down. Fold the side points in half to make the legs.

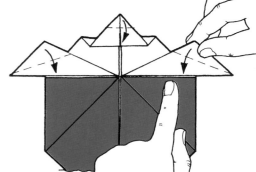

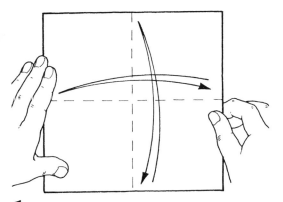

1 Fold and unfold the opposite sides together.

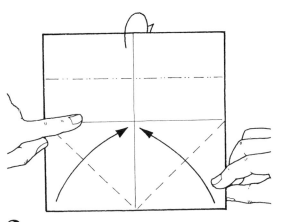

2 Fold the bottom corners in to the middle. Fold the top edges behind to meet the middle fold line.

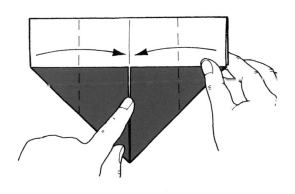

3 Fold the sides in to meet the middle fold line.

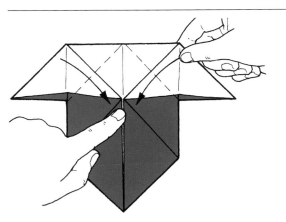

5 into triangles, as shown. Fold each half of the top edge down to meet the middle line.

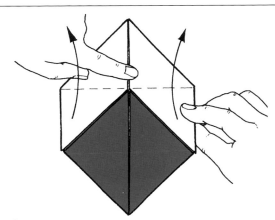

6 Fold the points up.

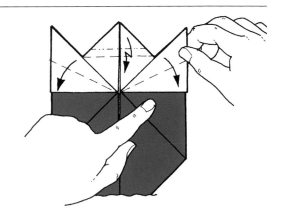

7 Fold the points out to either side. Fold the middle point down and back up.

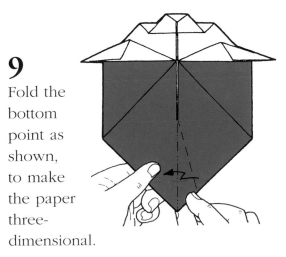

9 Fold the bottom point as shown, to make the paper three-dimensional.

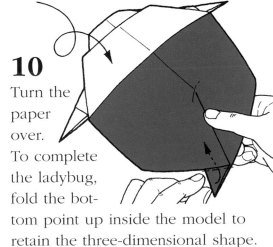

10 Turn the paper over. To complete the ladybug, fold the bottom point up inside the model to retain the three-dimensional shape.

Ladybugs have polka-dotted wings. Draw the spots on yours, or start out with a square of dotted paper.